House Cleaning Business

Get Started Today and Enjoy the Freedom of Being Your Own Boss

© **Copyright 2020 - All rights reserved.**

The content contained within this book may not be reproduced, duplicated, or transmitted without direct written permission from the author or the publisher.

Under no circumstances will any blame or legal responsibility be held against the publisher, or author, for any damages, reparation, or monetary loss due to the information contained within this book, either directly or indirectly.

Legal Notice:

This book is copyright protected. It is only for personal use. You cannot amend, distribute, sell, use, quote or paraphrase any part, or the content within this book, without the consent of the author or publisher.

Disclaimer Notice:

Please note the information contained within this document is for educational and entertainment purposes only. All effort has been executed to present accurate, up to date, reliable, complete information. No warranties of any kind are declared or implied. Readers acknowledge that the author is not engaging in the rendering of legal, financial, medical, or professional advice. The content within this book has been derived from various sources. Please consult a licensed professional before attempting any techniques outlined in this book.

By reading this document, the reader agrees that under no circumstances is the author responsible for any losses, direct or indirect, that are incurred as a result of the use of the information contained within this document, including, but not limited to, errors, omissions, or inaccuracies.

Table of Contents

Introduction v

Chapter 1: Setting Up Your Company 1

    Conducting Extensive Market Research
and Competitive Analysis 2
Writing Your Business Plan............................... 10

**Chapter 2: Creating Your Budget and
            Sourcing for Funds**.................................17

    Self-Funding... 18
Investor-Funding... 19
Accessing a Business Loan 21
Calculating the Startup Cost of
Your Business 22
Create a Break-Even Analysis 28
Securing Loans and Attracting Investors 29
Estimating the Profit Window 29
Startup Cost Worksheet for House
Cleaning Business.. 31

Chapter 3: Choosing Your Location and Structuring Your Business 34

Structuring Your Business 36

Chapter 4: Registering Your Business and Getting a Federal and State Tax ID Number 45

Registering Your Business with Federal Agencies 47

Registering Your Business with State Agencies 48

Getting Federal and State Tax ID Numbers 52

Chapter 5: Marketing and Creating Awareness 55

Conclusion 61

Introduction

A messy environment is profitable. If you previously looked at garbage and untidiness with disapproval, this message is for you: "Relax, you are looking at an opportunity to make some money." Untidiness exists for your benefit (that is if you understand how to harness this benefit). While many people want to become entrepreneurs, a quarter of them are certain of the businesses they want to invest in. If you are among the 1/3 who lack ideas of which business to go into, then this book is for you.

This book teaches you how to start a house cleaning business, a gainful venture where you turn the mess people make of their homes into profit. This reality is called "profitable messiness." Profitable messiness stops you from getting that imminent summons to the bankruptcy court while also providing adequate funding for your business. It protects your financial interests and reduces the number of times your customers make painful trips to the doctor. And with the financial benefits it promises, you gain control. Profitable messiness allows you to become your boss, and by working for the community, you create employment for others.

Experts tell everyone to rest and de-stress. They tell them spend their weekends amidst crazy funfair to reenergize for the coming week. They tell everyone to put their feet up and watch the news. But you didn't know that the arrangement everyone makes to rest their bodies is engineered, albeit indirectly, to make you rich. That's why I wrote this book; to remind you not to miss out on the business opportunities that other people's mess will bring you. And if you didn't know about these opportunities already, I will tell you.

Taking time off hectic schedules to allow the body to rest is cool, and while the rest is on-going, the owners of these bodies make a mess of their resting place; their homes. Since they are resting and making a mess, who cleans after them and who makes money from cleaning after them? You! You take their mess and turn it into the fifth mint. But the only thing is that this mint will be yours. And to mint your dollars, you won't be working with machines, plates, and paper but with soap, mops, and towels. You will be working with a business plan, a target market, a proper and cost-friendly licensing. And while you are at it, you should not ignore the importance of insurance and solid marketing strategies. You will give yourself and your business a professional attitude, the right staffing, coupled with the right tools and training for the job.

If you have ever been anxious over what business to start with a small capital, you need not fret anymore. This book is your go-to guide to starting a house cleaning business. Unlike some other startups that are capital intensive, a house cleaning business offers you the best return on investment with a low startup cost. If you understand the intricacies of this business, you will enjoy your work as you earn. And this is the good part.

Starting a home cleaning business will not push you down the labyrinth of burnout syndrome. You don't spend every day at a desk, at a, quite frankly, boring 9-5 job and listening to your colleagues complaining about everyone and everything. You get to control your resources and your time. If you have been losing sleep over what business to set up, worry no more. A house cleaning business will give you value for your effort. And you are going to see how you will make this happen through this book.

Chapter 1:

Setting Up Your Company

Starting your house cleaning service is not so different from setting up a pizza or ribs delivery service or any other service. To set up your company, you need to establish a feasible budget and work with that budget. Budgets are easy to set, but a handful of people know how to stick to their budgets. Setting a budget for business requires a minimal financial understanding of which one of the first lessons is the ability to draw a line between your personal and business funds. Many people lump their personal and business monies together. They get confused over what money belongs where and for what. Once you can separate your finances and pin them to a particular need, you have taken the first step toward setting up your company.

Starting your company is one of the exciting things you can do in your life. It gives you the mindset and power of a creator, and your obsession will be not to fail. There are key steps to setting up your company, and these steps are necessary if you want to prevent a crash. The steps involve planning, making sound financial decisions, and performing a series of legal activities. Let's take a run down the steps.

Conducting Extensive Market Research and Competitive Analysis

You have taken the first step to success, which is deciding to start a house cleaning service. That is an intelligent decision. But you should know that you aren't the only one who conceived this idea, and you should also know that there are other house cleaning services already operating before you made your decision. Despite these uncontrollable challenges and competition, one thing that can help you to stand out is your ability to identify the uniqueness you can bring to the table. Customers need to know why they should buy your services instead of continuing with the established names they are already buying from. Your ability to sway their minds, tantalize the taste buds, and change the decisions of available customers depends on your marketing and delivery strategies.

You cannot deliver quality service if you don't understand the behavior of your potential customers. This knowledge is closely tied to consumer behavior. And to use this to your advantage, you must understand the market. Every successful business thrives on the availability of willing and able customers. Market research is your ability to establish the presence and availability of customers for your business. This means that for every product, goods, or services you offer for sale at a given time and place, you must ensure that there are willing and able customers who are ready to buy your services. Let's say that, as a resident of Colorado, you want to set up a walk-in beauty shop that will cater to the hair and skin needs of African American women. A comprehensive market survey should tell you to choose either Aurora, Denver, Fort Morgan, or Colorado Springs for your business. But if you choose to set up shop in places like Cherry Hills Village, Woodland Park, Berthoud, or Windsor, you will end up shooting yourself in the leg. Why should you choose Aurora or Denver? It's because these places are densely populated with African Americans. Thus you will have willing and able customers in abundance.

When you have decided on where to set up your business, and after conducting extensive market research, you should consider carrying out a competitive analysis. Since Aurora is predominantly African, it's obvious that there will be existing beauty shops attending to the needs of the neighborhood women. So what should you do to ensure you attract and hold the attention of potential customers? You do a competitive analysis. You will have to discover the weakness or the shortsightedness of your competitors, and, effectively, use it to your advantage.

Market research and competitive analysis are a combination that helps startups to find a vantage point for their young and small businesses. If you want to set up a house cleaning service in Minnesota, you will have to study how other house cleaning services like Clean Touch Inc, Professional Home Cleaning LLC, and Maids in Minnesota function. Studying and analyzing their operational method is gainful for your business. And by doing this, you identify the uniqueness you should bring to the table. Market research and competitive analysis are the first steps to starting your business.

1. Conducting research enables you to understand the link between consumer behavior and economic trends. This knowledge increases any ideas you might come up with as regards providing the quality and nature of services your customers will need, instead of forcing the ones you think they should need on them. Understanding your consumer base (their tastes and expectations) from the beginning helps you not to make avoidable mistakes and reduces the frequency of unnecessary risks you might take.

2. You can weigh the available opportunities in the market. Understanding the opportunities is crucial because they will guard your decisions. They will also spell out the possible limitations in black and white. This way, you wouldn't be walking into a mess. Rather you will be cleaning the mess for a handsome fee. Understanding limitations to business can include knowing the population data based on age, wealth, family dynamics, and personal interests. To understand this barrier and to know how

to work with the data you have, to benefit your business, is the first step you must take if you want to start and grow a thriving house cleaning business. Let's assume you want to start your house cleaning business in Los Angeles; choosing neighborhoods like Malibu, Hidden Hills, Pacific Palisades, or Topanga means that your prices have to reek of class. The rich, white residents of these plush neighborhoods might turn their noses up at your services if an average American can afford them. The rich tend to believe that wealth buys a quality lifestyle, and if it's not expensive, it means it's tacky. So when you do market research, also study the dynamics of the environment you are going to be providing house cleaning services for. This will inform your decisions when you begin to provide the right and most efficient services for your customers based on their age, wealth, and personal or family interest.

3. You will have answers to the most basic questions regarding startups such as:

- The demand for your cleaning services: This will prevent any wastage of funds. Let's assume you have a limited budget; thus, you would want to start small, rake in dollars, and expand to richer neighborhoods. If you choose Colorado as your location, you might have to pay less attention to student dominated neighborhoods such as some parts of Denver, Durango, Fort Collins, Boulder, Golden, and Greely. It is unlikely for students to require house cleaning services. Everyone knows that most of them are paying their way through college with the help of student loans. And as such, they are hardly the available market you should be looking at.

- The size of the available market: This addresses the number of people that will need your services. The demand for your services is often conditioned by the size of the market. Thus, when choosing the location for your house cleaning service, always go for places with the highest number of willing and able customers. The size of the market is not determined by population, but by willingness, readiness, and ability of the population.

- The economic indicator that will condition your service: Knowing this gives you an idea of the income range and the employment rate of your prospective customers. Unemployed people or people who are not gainfully employed might trash the idea of outsourcing their house cleaning chores. Who would want to burn their lean budget on house cleaning services when they can use the soap and mop themselves?

- The location of your business: Where do you want to set up your business? Where do your customers live? How far can your business reach? You should have the answers to these questions ready.

- The nature of the market and how you can fit in: This takes you back to competitive analysis. You should study the market in your preferred location and establish the number and the efficiency of available options to customers. The study should explain how saturated the market is, and it should indicate the window of opportunity to enter the market.

- The general price the customers are already used to: If the environment has alternatives to the services you are offering, you already know that they are used to a certain price. What you decide to do with pricing determines the growth or decline of your business.

Pricing is the point where most startups encounter challenges. If you already have competitors in your chosen location, to get the right deal for you and your customers, you can organize a street interview or pick people randomly to fill-out questionnaires. The questions asked should address their satisfaction with and their expectations of the cleaning services available to them, it should address what they think of the pricing, and it should tackle the necessary steps the providers can take to make things easier for everyone. You should know that running a house cleaning business is not like every other business. Here, you are dealing with your customers directly; thus, their opinion matters. In this business, your focus should be to please your customers. You can achieve this by getting into their heads to know what they expect from your service.

Writing Your Business Plan

Your business plan is the roadmap that takes you to your destination. It will determine the success or failure of your business. Your business plan should resonate with what you arrived at after carrying out extensive market research and competitive analysis. A feasible business plan should structure your startup and should also explain the tools to use in running and growing that same business by doing the following:

- It should guide you through each stage of starting, structuring, and managing your business. It is your only way to see the take-off of your business and its landing.

- It should paint a clear picture of your funding both now and in the future, and it should also make space for future partnerships and expansion. If you write a business plan that provides house cleaning services for the residents of Colorado, you should include opportunities for expansion. Let's say a few years after starting your business in Colorado; you decide to expand to Wyoming, Nebraska, Kansas, and Oklahoma; your business plan will determine the smoothness or roughness of this expansion. And if, after a few years of running a blossoming house cleaning business in Colorado, you decide to source for an investor, the nature of your business plan will determine how possible this will be.

- It should be written in a way that meets your needs. There are two common categories of writing a business plan: the traditional and the lean startup. The traditional startup business plan is commonly used. It requires a standard structure and allows you to be detailed in each section. While the lean startup business plan is less common, but also uses a standard structure. Unlike the traditional startup business plan that will require elaboration, which could run into lengthy pages, the lean startup business plan summarizes key points and the most important elements of the business. The lean startup business plan takes a little time to write, and it is usually presented in a page or two.

If you have the hope to expand your business, or you will want investors to come in, the traditional startup business plan should be preferred. But if you want to start and see how it goes, you should work with the lean startup business plan. You are advised to use the traditional startup business plan for immediate or future expansion because investors or lenders often request this plan before they can part with their money. But if you are the one funding your business, going with the lean startup business plan is ideal. Every business plan has sections. While some insist on having all the accepted sections in their business plan, it is only necessary to include the sections that will put your house cleaning business in perspective. The sections of a traditional startup business plan are as follows:

1. Executive Summary: This section talks about the mission and vision of your company. It gives an idea of how successful your company will be. It also gives basic information about your organization, such as location, leadership team, and staffing. And if you intend to reach out to investors, the executive summary should contain the financial information of your company.

2. Company Description: This will include the problem your company is going to solve and why people should buy the services it will offer for sale. It should also give a list of the areas your company will be offering house cleaning services to. When these have been captured, you should include what you discovered to be your competitive advantage. Remember that knowing the edge you have over your competitors keeps you in line with your vision and mission statement. Well, your goal should never be to deliver any service less than the best.

3. Organization and Management: This is where you will pen down the legal structure of your business. After weighing your financial options and what could be done about them, you should choose a business structure that will protect your outfit and give it the exact balance of legal protections and benefits. We will discuss this extensively under the business structure. For management, if you are going to be working with other people, you should use an organizational chart to lay out the hierarchy in your company. If you are starting huge and you want to cover all of Colorado and reach out to most of the cities in Wyoming, Nebraska, and Kansas, you already know that you'll need help with the management. In this section of your traditional startup business plan, you will assign managerial roles to qualified assistants.

4. Marketing and Sales: This is the heart of your business. If you put every other thing in place, and you don't consider your marketing and sales strategy, your business might not succeed as you would want it to. You should establish who or where your market is, and when you have, also draw the roadmap to deliver your services to them effectively. Thus, to have a solid marketing and sales strategy, you must incorporate the findings from the market research and competitive analysis you made.

5. Funding: If you aren't the sole financer of your house cleaning business, this section should tackle the challenges of funding. If you prefer investors or you want to take a loan to start and grow your company, you must consider the legal and business aspect of it. You must be certain of the financial steps you want to take to avoid mistakes. You must also weigh your options before making any financial risks. This section would tackle the funding you will need and for how long you will need it before the business starts yielding profit and funding itself. It should also give a breakdown of how the fund will be used.

Unlike the typical business plan where you will need to have other sections, like financial projections and appendix, your traditional startup business plan for starting a house cleaning company might not need all that information. The reason is, you are using this as a roadmap to guide you through the journey of starting your company. It gives you focus and points you towards a definite direction.

If you want to start small and expand as the business grows, you should consider using the lean startup business plan. This plan allows you to change your strategy or refine your business along the way. The lean startup business plan has many versions, but the most commonly used is The

Business Model Canvas, which was developed by Alex Osterwalder. The components of this version will help you plan your small startup in the following steps:

1. Key partnership
2. Key activities
3. Key resources
4. Value proposition
5. Customer relationships
6. Customer segments
7. Channels
8. Cost structure
9. Revenue streams

Chapter 2:

Creating Your Budget and Sourcing for Funds

As a startup, you should create a budget that will take care of licenses, permits, your initial cleaning products, logistics, and advertising. If you are going to be the CEO and the pioneer staff, you might save funds that would have gone into hiring labor. But if you think you might want one or more people to work with you, you will have to include labor in your budget. Having a clear-cut budget will help determine the extent of funding you will require for your business.

The financial needs of every business differ; that's why there is no specific solution to funding for startups. If you have been planning to be your own boss for a while, the chances are that you might be saving for the business. If you are, the nature of funding available for your business will not be the same as that of another who has no personal funds set aside for business. Therefore, your financial situation and your vision for the company will determine the nature and type of funding you will access for your company. It will also go a long way in conditioning the financial future of your business. Thus, when you agree on the much startup funding your business requires, the way to source for it becomes clear to you. There are three basic ways to fund businesses.

Self-Funding

This type of funding, also known as bootstrapping, allows you to leverage your financial resources to start and grow your business. This doesn't necessarily mean that the money must come from your savings. It refers to any fund you access for your business, which has no legal attachment. Here, you can access soft loans from family and friends. Self-funding, when it is not coming from your pocket, rarely attracts interest, and the lenders do not always emphasize specific deadlines. This is the most comfortable funding style, but it also has its risks. Sometimes entrepreneurs who favor this funding lose sight of the bigger picture. This might be because they have no lender breathing down on them, or they have no fear of pending or imminent court ruling.

Investor-Funding

This involves legalities, but it is an effective way you could fund your house cleaning business. If you want to start big, as we mentioned earlier, where you provide cleaning services for more cities, you would need an investor (if you are unable to fund the company). The investor will provide money for your business in the form of venture capital investment. This kind of capital is offered by investors in exchange for part ownership and control in the business. Therefore, you should understand that venture capital is not a loan, and there is no form of loan servicing with it. Instead, it is ideal for high-growth companies, for example, those that want to start big and continue to expand quickly, as it favors the higher risks involved in exchange for higher returns on the investment. It also anticipates a longer investment window.

If you would prefer to access venture funding for your business, you should follow these steps:

1. Source for an investor. While on this, look for an individual investor (angel investors) or look for venture capital firms. If you go for the latter option, do not ignore the importance of background checks. Some venture capital firms are not reputable, and some of them do not have the necessary experience of working with startup companies. You need to make such checks because you won't want to make avoidable mistakes.

2. Present your business plan to them. An investor will want to see your business plan to be certain of profit before they invest their money.

3. Walk the investor through your startup business plan.

4. Work out the terms of funding with them. When you do this, ensure you understand the process. At this point, you can get an advocate or a broker involved in the process.

5. Work out the terms and legalities of the business with them. This is the moment you should be careful. Some investors are fraudulent, and

if you aren't careful, they might smuggle in some dubious clauses in the agreement. Such clauses (backed by law) can affect your position in your own company.

Accessing a Business Loan

If you are unable to self-fund your business and if you don't want to share ownership or control of your business with a third party, you should consider getting a business loan. For you to access a business loan from any of the Small Business Administration (SBA) approved bodies, you will need a business plan. You will also need an expense sheet, and you will come up with a feasible financial projection for at least the next five years. Your business plan, your expense sheet, and your future financial projections will give you an idea of how much you will need to start your business and run it for an estimated period. If you are going to apply for loans, you will need to use the traditional startup business plan format. This is because you'll need to assure the bank that funding your business is one of the smart moves they will make. And once you have your business plan and expense sheet ready, you should contact the banks to get the first and most crucial stage of your business started.

The United States has a body that helps entrepreneurs get funding for their businesses. Hence if you opt for funding through loans, you might have to consider applying for SBA guaranteed loans. Small Business Administration guaranteed loans help you secure traditional loans from banks. If you have trouble securing loans from banks, applying for such loans through Small Business Administration guaranteed loans assures the lenders of your credibility and eligibility for the loan. Once we have tackled the issue of funding, we will move on to the next stage, which is to calculate the startup cost of your business before you begin.

Calculating the Startup Cost of Your Business

To calculate the startup cost of your house cleaning business, you have to answer two key questions: who do you want to provide house cleaning services for, and in what magnitude do you want to provide these services? These questions will help you figure out the startup cost for your business, and in calculating it, the following will be explained:

1. How you can identify startup expenses.
2. How you can identify the cost of your expenses.
3. How you can add up your expenses to get a comprehensive financial pattern.
4. How you can utilize your knowledge of startup cost calculation to source for startup funds.

In identifying the startup expenses of your business, you need to pay attention to what your business does, determined by the category it falls under. This identification is necessary, considering the nature of most businesses. There are three categories of businesses: brick and mortar businesses, online businesses, and service providers. Brick and mortar businesses make use of physical offices where customers and clients can walk in and have their needs attended to.

Online businesses function by the name; they are virtual businesses that offer their products and services through digital means. Although their presence is mostly felt online, such businesses also have physical offices they operate from.

Online businesses like Amazon, AliExpress, eBay, Walmart, Best Buy, Target, Etsy, Home Depot, and Macy's offer their services digitally, although they have a physical presence too. Dropshipping and other forms of e-commerce also fall under this category. And for service providers such as organizations that provide network, cleaning, storage, and processing services for consumers directly, they offer the kind of services anyone will consider intangible. AT&T, Verizon Communications, T-Mobile, Airbnb, Asana, Microsoft, LinkedIn, and Facebook are among the companies that offer digital services. The companies under this category provide consumers with services they can access online, such as internet service providers, telephone companies, outsourced services suppliers, and content providers (digital services providers such as the services buyers can access on Fiverr and Upwork).

These businesses include personal services, business services, marketing, and sales services, home services, computer and technology services, children's services, and events services. Among these businesses under services, house cleaning businesses fall under home services. And it will interest you to know that each category determines the startup expenses of the businesses under it.

When you are done identifying your startup expenses, you should draw an estimated cost. This list should contain the total of what you have identified. To begin, you should have a list of possible financial commitments. When you draw your list of possible expenses, you should know that while some things may have a fixed price, such as the money to hire an office space and the money that will be used to acquire permits, licenses, and money to pay other fees; others won't.

These expenses are defined, but initial costs such as money that will go into buying cleaning agents and cleaning equipment and money to pay employee salaries might not be fixed. Other expenses are not definite. And you need to put these into consideration when drawing your expenses. This is how to do it. When you come up with the estimated and actual prices of the things you need to buy and the things you will likely spend money on, you should put some money aside for additional/unforeseen expenses. But when funding is limited, you might consider eliminating some expenses.

When you establish what you will be spending money on and how much, then you have reached the last phase of calculating your startup costs. What you should do is to divide your expenses into two categories: one-off expenses and monthly expenses. In house cleaning business (and since the business is not capital intensive), most of the expenses are recurrent. That's why even though you might spend a certain amount of money to acquire the initial permit, licenses, and insurance; you will need to spend subsequent sums to renew these things. In the house cleaning business, expenditures like these are categorized under one-time expenses. This is the same as investing in capital intensive machinery for production. These machines are fixed, but they require maintenance to function well.

One-off expenses are the initial costs required to start a business. These can cover money used to register your business, the money you spend to design your business logo, and the money you pay to have your business on local listings. When you have this readily calculated, you should add it up to your monthly expenses. Your monthly expenses should include money spent on variables like employee salaries, rents, utility bills, and transportation. And when you are calculating your startup costs, you should calculate your expenses based on a five-year projection. This will give you a clear picture of the right amount of funding you need and how soon you need it.

When you are through with adding your financial expenses, you can proceed to the last item on the list: using your startup calculation to get startup funding for your business. This part has been mentioned while creating a traditional startup business plan. When you sum your expenses together, ensure the representation is accurate, clear, and precise. Investors and lenders will be interested in this part. The way you capture your calculation will determine investor's or lender's interest in the business. They will want to see what profit awaits them in the venture. Remember, their interest is in return on their investment. Thus, your calculated startup cost will reveal and explain this to them. There are other details your calculation should reveal to investors and lenders. They need these details to decide whether to go ahead with you or not. We will elaborate on these details in the following headings.

Create a Break-Even Analysis

Investors and lenders are looking forward to seeing how well you captured this in your calculation. This will address how much money you will invest in the business at the initial stage. This money is expected to take care of labor, the initial products and equipment for cleaning, the money to go into hiring office spaces (assuming your company will be a brick and mortar business), and the money that will go into maintaining an online presence. If your company is more virtual than actual, you might invest more funds in running online ads and paying social media marketers. This doesn't mean that offline businesses do not need to have a strong online presence. Rather, it means that the online visibility of your business will increase with running an online business. The money that will go into doing this should be considered when you calculate the startup cost of your business before you begin.

Securing Loans and Attracting Investors

If you will need investors or prefer to acquire a business loan from venture capital firms, when calculating the startup cost of your business, you should take into account the means to achieve these things. And if you are using personal funds to start your business before sourcing for investors, you should weigh the financial benefits and consequences of self-funding and investor funding.

Estimating the Profit Window

When you calculate the startup cost of your business, you should project the expenses and funding period. A lot of people do not understand the demands and restrictions of setting up a business – that's why some of them begin to take away a huge amount of money from their business even when their financing isn't stable enough. To avoid making this popular mistake, you need to separate personal funds from business funds, and you need to give your business the right time and space to stand on its own before dipping your hand into the business purse. This is the time that will enable it to cover the startup expenses and yield the desired profit. When you consider these when calculating startup costs, your business will be stable enough to pay off loans (assuming you took some), use the fund itself, and start yielding profit.

Calculating your house cleaning startup cost before you begin is the key that will unlock a profit-filled future and a mind-blowing success for your business. There are a few basic startup costs you will encounter in your business, and these costs are not dependent on the category your business falls under. This means that, even if you want your house cleaning business to be based online because you do not have enough money to pay for office space, you must consider expenses like equipment and supply, communications, and utilities. You will have to store your working tools somewhere, and if that isn't your basement, you will have to pay for storage or parking space. You will have to pay for licenses and permits, insurance, employee salaries, marketing ads, market research, legalities, inventory, and you will pay for the processes that will start your online presence. We have done a lot of talking; now, we will see how to draw a startup cost for a house cleaning business.

Startup Cost Worksheet for House Cleaning Business

This worksheet is a feasible calculation for a house cleaning business. It has been used here to explain what this chapter is about further. If you want to calculate your startup costs, you should use this as a guide rather than for exactness. This means that when you calculate yours, pay attention to the current market trends. The worksheet contains two tables comprised of three columns. The first table has the one-off expenses, budget, and actual cost, while the second contains the monthly expenses, budget, and actual expenses. The budget in each table is an estimated amount entered during the calculation, and when you have acquired these things, you should enter the exact amount spent on each item in the "actual cost" column. Below the tables is another column for the sum of funds required. What you should enter in this column are the estimated, calculated costs. This is what the investor or lender will be looking to see. Do not wait till the items have been acquired before you come up with the total amount of funds required.

HOUSE CLEANING BUSINESS

One-off Expenses	Budget	Actual Cost
Rent		
Security deposit	1,500.00	
First month's rent	1,700.00	
First month's utilities and bills (internet and phone connections)	300.00	
Improvement costs		
Computer, vacuum machines, uniforms, and stationery	1,500.00	
Tables and furniture	1,350.00	
Mops, buckets, soaps, brushes and dustpan, towels, duster, protective gloves, baking soda, white vinegar, oils, and microfiber cleaning cloths	800.00	
Essentials		
Kitchen and lavatory cleaning tools	1,400.00	
Indoor cleaning tools	500.00	
Outdoor cleaning tools	600.00	
Miscellaneous		
Licenses and permits	200.00	
Legal fees	250.00	
Insurance	400.00	
Technology	400.00	
Software	300.00	
Total funds required	**11,200.00**	**0.00**

HOUSE CLEANING BUSINESS

Monthly Expenses	Budget	Actual Cost
Rent		
Monthly rent	1,350.00	
Property insurance	4oo.00	
Utilities	300.00	
Employees		
Payroll	4,000.00	
Payroll taxes	1,150.00	
Health insurance	700.00	
Professional services		
Accounting	300.00	
Legal	200.00	
Consultants	250.00	
Other	100.00	
Supplies		
Office supplies	500.00	
cleaning supplies	1000.00	
Marketing		
Digital ads	250.00	
Promotional materials	350.00	
Miscellaneous		
Liability insurance	350.00	
Purchases, repairs, and maintenance	250.00	
Organizational dues	50.00	
Total monthly expenses	**11,500.00**	**0.00**
Total funds required 22,700.00		

Chapter 3:

Choosing Your Location and Structuring Your Business

The location of your business is important. It will determine the taxes you will pay, and it will also determine the growth or decline of your business based on zoning laws and other regulations. That's why before you carry out market research or competitive analysis, you should choose your location first. To reiterate, choosing a location is strategic to the growth of your business, and you should make your choice based on the most favorable state, city, and neighborhood. When conducting detailed research on where to locate your business, always remember that you will need to register it, you will pay taxes and that you will need to acquire licenses and permits. The laws and regulations of the location will either restrict your business or help expand it. Thus, after calculating your startup cost, consider the nature of expenses within the location and the impact these expenses will have on your funds.

Since you will be providing direct service to your customers, it is important to consider the factors that control businesses in different states. In the United States, every state and the cities that make up these states have laws governing startups. Therefore when you choose the location for your business, have these in mind:

a. Your location will determine the tax you will pay.
b. It will determine the zoning laws and regulations your business will be subjected to. This will include property values, rental rates, business insurance rates, utilities, licensing, and fees.
c. If you have employees, the laws and regulations will determine the salaries you pay. Most states insist that employees be paid standard salaries. Thus when choosing a location, consider the minimum wage laws of the place.

Minimum wage law is not the only law to consider when choosing a location for your business.

You should also consider zoning laws and how your business might be affected by them. If you intend to buy, rent, or build an office space, it is ideal you check out the zoning requirements of the area and ensure your office abides by it. Some neighborhoods are strictly residential or are forbidden to accommodate certain kinds of businesses. And if you erroneously think that your house cleaning business can be located anywhere because it is house cleaning, you might have another think coming.

If you are the sole proprietor, with one or more staff, and you want to work from your own home, you must check out the zoning requirements of your area to know if you are permitted to run businesses from home. Having this knowledge and sticking to the rules is important, and because you are meeting public demands, you should be law-abiding as much as you can. We will discuss the intricacies of the next heading based on the points mentioned above.

Structuring Your Business

When you are making inquiries into zoning laws, also look into tax regulations for the locations you have picked. Some states are popular for enacting favorable tax laws and environments that favor some kinds of startups. Since your house cleaning business is not capital intensive, its tax landscape might not be all that tough. After deciding on location based on these premises, you should go right ahead to structure your business.

How you structure your business will affect how much tax you pay, your ability to raise money, and the paperwork you need to file during the process of registering it, and it will also affect your liability. It is ideal to choose the structure your business will run on before you register it with the federal or state government. When you register your business, you will be given a tax ID number and all the required permits.

When choosing a location and business structure, consider the possibility of conversion and expansion. If, after a few years, you decide to introduce an investor or increase funding through venture capital firms, you should consider this when choosing the structure of your business. There are certain restrictions placed on some business structures, and when you choose to do, otherwise, your business might suffer unsavory consequences like tax problems and foreclosure. Therefore to avoid encountering such problems, you should consult business counselors, attorneys, and accountants before you structure your business. There are different ways to structure your business. Read on to discover them.

Sole Proprietorship

This is synonymous with self-funding: it is the easiest way to start a business, and it gives you total control of your business. According to the point raised by Small Business Administration, you are considered a sole proprietor if there is no difference between you and your business. This means that your business assets and liabilities are the same as your assets and liabilities. If you start a house cleaning business that is directly linked to you, as a sole proprietor, you can be petitioned or arraigned for the debts and financial failures of the business. If you register your business as a sole proprietor, it will be quite difficult to raise money from external sources for your business. Banks and investors rarely consider sole proprietors for investment. Structuring your business this way becomes advantageous if you want to test your entrepreneurial ability before starting big. It favors those who want to start small with less risk.

Partnership

This is also like investor-funding: you collaborate with someone else to fund and run your business. A partnership is considered the easiest/simplest business structure. It comprises two or more people. If you want to include others into your business but want to retain overall control, you should go for a limited partnership. A limited partnership has one general partner with unlimited liability and unlimited control, while other partners will have limited liability and limited control.

And these details will be duly documented in the partnership agreement. Taxes are based on personal tax returns, and the general partner with unlimited liability pays self-employment tax. There is another form of partnership called limited liability partnership. Unlike the limited partnership where the general partner has unlimited control over the business, partners in limited liability partnerships have limited liability in the business.

This means that no partner is held responsible for the actions of other partners. The laws guiding limited liability partnership protects them from this. Both forms of partnership are good, and each has a peculiar advantage. While the limited partnership allows the general partner to retain unlimited control over the business, it does not offer protection for the general partner to be exempted from the consequences of the actions of other partners.

Limited Liability Company (LLC)

A limited liability company operates like the name: it protects your personal you from the business you. If perchance, you operate an LLC, and your company encounters huge financial losses, your personal life will not suffer the consequences of the fall of your business. This means that your assets, such as your vehicles, house, and savings account, will not be at risk when your business faces great financial difficulties. And if you need to offset the financial burden of your business through your account, you won't bother with paying corporate taxes. But the downside of this structure is that since members of limited liability companies are considered self-employed, they pay self-employment taxes towards Medicare and Social Security.

When choosing LLC as your business structure, you should consider the laws of the location. In some states, when members of an LLC exits the company or when new members join, the company is mandated by law to dissolve and re-form another structure based on the new membership. But this can be overlooked if the partnership agreement stated that ownership could be sold or transferred. If you have significant personal assets, LLC is the right structure for your business. This structure protects you from paying a higher tax rate, unlike the rates required for a corporation.

Corporation

This structure offers better legal and financial protection to its owners. Often called a C corp, members who are a part of this structure are protected from legal actions taken against the company. Corporations can be taxed, and they can also be held legally liable. The advantage members in a corporation stand to enjoy is that their assets are protected from corporate liability. But the downside (if it could be considered one) is that the cost of setting up corporations is higher when compared to other structures.

Corporations also require extensive record-keeping, operational processes, and reporting. If you want to get around paying taxes legally, then structuring your business as a corporation wouldn't be ideal because, unlike sole proprietors, partnerships, and LLCs, corporations pay income tax on their profit. This is stressful, right? But that's not all. Sometimes, the income profit of corporations gets taxed twice: when the company makes a profit, and when the dividends of tax returns are paid into the personal account of the shareholders.

The reason for explaining all these in detail is to prepare you to make informed decisions when you want to structure your company. Corporations differ from Limited Liability Companies. In a corporation, when a shareholder leaves the company or sells their shares, their exit does not affect the company's functionality; rather, the company functions seamlessly as if nothing happened. Thus we have:

1. Business structure = sole proprietor – ownership = one person – liability = unlimited personal liability – taxes = personal tax required.
2. Business structure = Partnership – ownership – two or more persons – liability = unlimited personal liability (which can be changed if structured as a limited partnership) – taxes = self-employment tax (but could change for limited partners) – the tax is personal.
3. Business structure = Limited Liability Company (LLC) – ownership = One or more persons – liability = business bears the financial loses – taxes = it could be self-employment tax, personal tax, or corporate tax. All three taxes could be infused at some point.
4. Business structure = corporation - C corp – ownership = one or more persons, but would not exceed 100 persons, and they must be US citizens – liability = owners or shareholders are not liable for the company – taxes = personal tax.

When you look at the structure above, you will choose the one suitable for your business. Startups are often encouraged to structure their business according to available funds and their dream for the business. Even though Facebook and Airbnb are global names and are accessed from different countries, the reality is that not all startups would want to become global names. Some might prefer to remain locally relevant. A person who has spent almost all their life in Alabama or Detroit might decide to start a house cleaning company and not want it to expand into other states. This does not make their dreams less valid than others who do want to expand through the United States.

Now, if you desire to start and run a house cleaning business within your locality, after putting the state laws and regulations into strict consideration, you should choose the sole proprietor structure for your business. This will be of immense benefit if you are operating on a low budget. This way, you get to conserve resources and use them for the most important things.

Chapter 4:

Registering Your Business and Getting a Federal and State Tax ID Number

Once you are done choosing location and business structure, the next step is to register your business and get a tax ID number. Every startup is expected to have a federal and state tax ID number. These numbers are valuable for different reasons and purposes. We will get into them shortly.

When registering your business, consider your location and business structure. When you have straightened these out nicely, you will hardly encounter any difficulties registering your business. If you prefer the sole proprietor structure, registering your business begins with choosing a business name. When you develop the idea to start a business, it is noteworthy to create a business name. And when you do that, you are advised to protect it by registering it with the appropriate agencies.

Choosing a business name is quite tedious, more tedious than picking the right outfit for an interview. A lot of name suggestions will pop-up in your head, and at every corner you turn, you will see ideas in everything. But amid your confusion and suggestions, you should have one fact in mind; choose a name that resonates with your brand. Your business identity matters. That's why you should choose a name that tells your potential customers what services you provide. Choosing a business name and registering it is crucial to starting a business. There are four ways to register your business name, and these ways are legally mandatory, depending on your business structure and location. The ways include:

a. **Entity Name:** This protects you at the state level.

b. **Trademark:** This is useful at the federal level.

c. **Doing Business As (DBA):** This does not give any form of legal protection, but it might be legally required in some cases.

d. Domain Name: This protects the website of your business.

These name registrations are independent, and they are legal. In some cases, small startups tend to use the same name for different registrations. But you should know that it isn't mandatory to do that. When you decide on the business name to use, it is your prerogative to choose which registration to go for. But each business name registration is dependent on the kind you want to get for your business. Although it is not compulsory to register your business, especially if you are using your legal name, the downside is that not registering your business can prevent you from enjoying liability protection, legal benefits, and tax benefits. We will look at the available forms of registering your business.

Registering Your Business with Federal Agencies

Not all businesses require registration with the federal government to become legal. While major business organizations such as the food companies register with the federal government, some small scale businesses need not do so. But if you want your house cleaning business to enjoy the trademark protection, you should consider registering with the federal government. If you want your house cleaning business to have the federal government trademark, you should file your brand or business name with the United States Patent and Trademark Office.

Registering Your Business with State Agencies

If you structured your business to be a partnership or a Limited Liability Company, you would have to register your business with the state government of your location. And if you expand to other states, you also need to register with the state government of those states. The only thing is that you may not have to pass through the process of registration. The ideal thing to do is to register with the state where you began and then file for foreign qualification. We will discuss this in a bit. To be qualified to have your business registered in any state, these criteria are required:

    a. Your business must be physically present in that state.

3. You should be ready to pay the official filing fee to have your business foreign qualified.

These three requirements must be met before your business becomes foreign qualified. But you should know that things change, and new laws are enacted. When you decide to expand, check with your state of formation and the state you want to expand to for the requirements and necessary fees. However, if you aren't seeking to get the qualified foreign status for your company, what you are required to do after structuring is to register. The fees needed to register your business vary with business structure, but the information you need to have your business registered is the same. To register your business, you will need:

1. Your business name.
2. The location of your business.
3. The ownership or management structure of your business.
4. The information of the registered agent you employed their services.
5. And the number and value of shares available. This information is required if your business is a corporation.

But the information listed above is not straight-jacket information. When you decide to register your business, the registered agent you work with will tell you the needed requirement according to state laws and the structure of your business.

Getting Federal and State Tax ID Numbers

The federal tax ID number, also known as Employers Identification Number (EIN) and your state tax ID numbers, are necessary for tax payment. This number works like your personal social security number but differs because the EIN secures your business instead of you. You need to get these numbers for your business because they enable you to pay federal and state taxes for your business. Your EIN enables you to do the following: pay federal taxes, hire employees, open a bank account, and apply for business licenses and permits. Applying for an EIN is free, and you are encouraged to go for it after registering your business. There are a few reasons why you need an EIN for your business, and they include:

a. You need it to pay your employees.

b. Your business activities should comprise in-person meetings with customers in the state.

c. A good portion of the revenue your business generates must come from the state.

d. A good number of your employees must be working within the state.

There are two ways to register your business with state agencies: you might register online, or you might be required to file paper documents personally or through the mail. There are offices where you can register your business with the state, and they are the Secretary of State's Office, the Business Bureau of the state, or the state's official Business Agency.

To have your business dully registered with the state government, you are required to work with a registered agent in the state to walk you through the registration process. The work of a registered agent is to receive the required official papers and legal documents for your company. This does not mean that you cannot register your company yourself. The thing is that many people prefer to use a registered agent to have their company registered with the state government.

If you start your business and get it dully registered in one state and later decide to expand to other states, you might need to file for a foreign qualification in other states where you are running your business. Filing for foreign qualification informs the state where you started your business that your business is domestic. Let's say that you formed your business in Colorado, and you decide to expand to Wyoming, Nebraska, Kansas, and Oklahoma. The Colorado state government will know that your business is domestic, and then the other states will know that you are operating a foreign business on their soil. You need to file for the foreign qualification because your business needs to pay taxes and other annual report fees in all the states where your business is operational.

You should know that not all active businesses in various states are recognized as foreign qualified. To have your business qualified, you should:

1. File a Certificate of Authority with the state.
2. Some states require a Certificate of Good Standing from your domestic state of operation; you are expected to have this.

b. You need it if you want to operate a partnership or corporation business structure.
c. You need it to file for tax returns.

For your state ID number, you should know that the obligations that come with tax payment vary according to state. Thus, you need to find out what your state laws say about income and employment taxes. You also need to know that taxes vary according to state based on employment insurance and workers' compensation insurance. Therefore before you file for a state ID number, find out if you are expected to pay tax. But state ID numbers are not needed for tax payment only. You can use it to protect yourself against identity theft, that's if your business is structured to be a sole proprietor.

Registering your business and getting a tax ID number is not the last thing required to complete the legalities required for your business. You need to get a permit or license to operate. Since we are discussing starting a house cleaning business, you need to get a state license and permit. Federal permits are required for business controlled by the federal government, and house cleaning is not among such businesses.

House cleaning businesses, including other businesses such as auctions, construction, plumbing, farming, retail, restaurants, and vending machines, are controlled by the state government. That's why for your house cleaning business, you need a state permit and licensing. You should also know that some permits and licenses expire within a period. As such, you should keep an eye on the expiry dates. If you default on renewal, your business can get shut down by the government. And to avoid telling this sorry tale, you should find out what your state, county, and city regulations are and stick to them. Once you have done these things, your house cleaning business is as good as ready.

Chapter 5:

Marketing and Creating Awareness

If you do all that has been mentioned so far without strategizing how to promote and protect your business, your business might not be as successful as the big guns in the house cleaning business industry. Even though, as a startup, you aren't competing with them, you need to create an awareness that gets your business plastered on the minds of the available market.

Many startups develop a solid business plan that should get them off the ground within a short period, but they end up going in circles. And after many months and years of activeness, their businesses still function like a startup. A lot could be responsible for this, of which lack of adequate or badly strategized awareness is one of. Hence, to learn from their mistakes and get your business off the ground in no time, you need to launch an aggressive and strategic awareness creation. How do you achieve this, especially if you are on a shoestring budget? Invest in marketing and advertisement.

A lot of people have made purchasing choices they wouldn't have if the producers of such products hadn't taken advertisements seriously. Check out the goings-on in Hollywood. Some movie producers understand the art of awareness creation; that's why they put their products at the exact place where potential customers will see them. This is the same as creating awareness for your house cleaning business. What do you do to ensure you capture the gaze and minds of your potential customers? It begins from the first thing they see or hear. If you choose visual or audio ads, you must ensure that you capture the senses of your potential customers within the first five seconds. It could be your logo, the inscription on your flier, or the jingles you choose. Whichever one you are working with, you should ensure it appeals to your potential customers while holding on to their attention.

There is something nice about creating awareness: it mustn't be expensive, but it should be tailored to arrest and retain the interest of your target audience. If you are on a tight budget, you can buy quality ads from virtual platforms such as Fiverr or Upwork. These platforms are great places to buy quality content at a lower price. Therefore, take advantage of the opportunity and grow your business. When you must have obtained the right ads for your business, the next step should be getting across to your target audience.

A lot of people use social media for different purposes, and apart from social interactions, social media is a great place to promote your business. We have Instagram and Facebook. These platforms are helping people to grow their businesses every day. When you throw your business doors open, you can promote your business through sponsored ads on Facebook. The cool part is that sponsored content on Facebook tracks potential customers through cookies. Thus when you sponsor Facebook ads templates tailored for your business, anyone who had searched for the services you offer on Google gets to see them. You can also create a Facebook page and invite your friends and family to like the page. This, too, works wonders.

You can promote your business on your website. You can recommend your visitors to sign up for your newsletter or request their permission to send popup notifications to them. You can promote your business through email marketing, popup ads, or google search to locate your potential customers.

You can also promote your business on local listings. Daily, thousands of people visit these platforms to check out new and trusted businesses whose services they can buy. If you add your business to local listings, you increase the visibility of your business and the possibility of reaching out to potential customers. Local listings available in the United States include Yelp, Thumbtack, Yellow Pages, Kudzu, Better Business Bureau, Manta, Judy's Book, CitySquares, USdirectory.com, Here, Local.com, Angie's List, MagicYellow, USCity, Yext, The Business Journals, Citysearch, Fave, BrownBook, Merchant Circle, Kompass, Superpages, EZlocal.com, MyHuckleberry, CityVoter, Craigslist, Volta, Akama, JustDail, AmericanTowns, eLocal, CityGrind, Ziplocal, Zidster, netHulk, LocalFolder.com, Insider Pages, and Switchboard.

When you have created enough awareness and must have begun business in earnest, encourage your customers to post positive reviews on your social media handles. You can publish your success stories on your Facebook page, but your customers should post positive reviews too. Your potential customers need to know that you didn't doctor the reviews and that you can deliver the services you claim you can. The idea is to publish your wins and also encourage your customers to post their satisfaction with your services.

When you render house cleaning services to people, encourage them to refer you. Potential customers trust the services they got to know about through referral. So if you want your business to grow in leaps and bounds through referral, endeavor to satisfy your customers. And when you are done with a particular job, maintain regulated communication with your customers.

We understand that some people can be touchy and might misunderstand your goodwill; therefore, to maintain a healthy customer relationship, you should inquire from them if you can keep in touch. If they approve of doing so, take advantage of it, and never allow another brand to come within their radar. Always remember that your customers are important; they hold the key to the growth of your business.

Conclusion

Starting a house cleaning business is about the easiest and one of the most profitable businesses you can run in the United States. This business is key to financial freedom because you have the strategies to start a lesser capital-intensive business that promises huge returns. As you create your business plan, choose your location, and perform the necessary legalities to get your business started and running, never forget or overlook the importance of creating awareness. If you record success in every aspect of starting your business but fail to create the right awareness of it, your business is as good as not started.

The point is to get started on your journey and build up your clientele base slowly but surely!

Wishing you the best in your future success.

www.ingramcontent.com/pod-product-compliance
Lightning Source LLC
Chambersburg PA
CBHW051539240526
45465CB00027B/729